Math with
Cars and Trucks
Measurement and Estimation

Ian F. Mahaney

PowerKiDS press™

New York

Published in 2013 by The Rosen Publishing Group, Inc.
29 East 21st Street, New York, NY 10010

First Edition

Editor: Joanne Randolph
Book Design: Greg Tucker

Photo Credits: Cover EvrenKalinbacak/Shutterstock.com; pp. 4–5 Monkey Business Images/Shutterstock.com; pp. 6–7 Peter Samuels/Photodisc/Getty Images; p. 8 Brand X Pictures/Getty Images; p. 9 Max Blain/Shutterstock.com; p. 10 Bogdanhoda/Shutterstock.com; p. 11 © Map Resources; p. 12 Beelde Photography/Shutterstock.com; pp. 13, 17 iStockphoto/Thinkstock; p. 14 (top) Jigkofoto/Shutterstock.com; p. 14 (bottom) N. Mitchell/Shutterstock.com; p. 15 Neil Roy Johnson/Shutterstock.com; p. 16 by Greg Tucker; pp. 18–19 Stephen Mallon/Taxi/Getty Images; pp. 20–21 Stanislaw Tokarski/Shutterstock.com.

Library of Congress Cataloging-in-Publication Data

Mahaney, Ian F.
 Math with cars and trucks : measurement and estimation / by Ian F. Mahaney. — 1st ed.
    p. cm. — (Core math skills)
 Includes index.
 ISBN 978-1-4488-9658-5 (library binding) — ISBN 978-1-4488-9774-2 (pbk.) —
 ISBN 978-1-4488-9775-9 (6-pack)
 1. Estimation theory—Juvenile literature. 2. Measurement—Juvenile literature. 3. Mathematical statistics—Juvenile literature. I. Title.
 QA276.13.M34 2013
 510—dc23
                                    2012026923

Manufactured in the United States of America

CPSIA Compliance Information: Batch #W13PK4: For Further Information contact Rosen Publishing, New York, New York at 1-800-237-9932

Contents

Estimating and Measuring

How much does your car weigh? You can **estimate** the weight by comparing your car to one for which you know the weight. A **similar**, but smaller, car weighs 2,500 pounds. Maybe you estimate that your car weighs 3,000 pounds.

You find out that your car weighs 1.5 tons. This is a **measurement**, or an exact amount found with a yardstick, scale, or other tool.

To see if your estimate is right, you will need to convert tons to pounds. If 1 ton = 2,000 pounds, then your math sentence would be:
1.5 tons x 2,000 pounds per ton = 3,000 pounds. Your estimate was correct! There are many ways to learn about estimating and measuring by using cars and trucks as examples.

Conversion Box
1 pound = .45 kilogram
1 ton = .9 metric ton

You could estimate how much your 3,000-pound car weighs with your family in it, too. If you know about how much each person weighs, just add each number to the 3,000 pounds.

A truck weighs 8 tons, and 1 ton equals 2,000 pounds. How many pounds does the truck weigh?

(See answers on p. 22)

Figure It Out

Getting Ready to Go

A family buys groceries at the supermarket and takes the bags home in their **antique** convertible. There is a rectangular space in the trunk that measures around 48 inches wide and is a bit more than 14 inches long.

The grocery bags measure 12 inches wide and 14 inches long. Arranged so that the 14-inch side of the bag fits in the 14-inch space in the trunk, you can estimate how many bags fit in the space. To do so, divide the **approximate** width of the trunk by the width of one bag:

48 inches ÷ 12 inches = 4 bags that will fit in the trunk.

Conversion Box
1 inch = 2.5 centimeters

You can use what you know about grocery bag widths to estimate the width of your trunk. Three grocery bags that are 12 inches wide fit side by side with a bit of space left, and you know that 3 x 12 inches = 36 inches. Now you know your trunk is about 40 inches wide.

How many suitcases that are 16 inches (41 cm) wide and 14 inches long fit in a trunk 48 inches wide and 14 inches long?

(See answers on p. 22)

Dare to Compare

Some trucks carry groceries on rectangular platforms called **pallets**. A grocery pallet measures 48 inches wide and 40 inches long. The **perimeter** of a pallet is found by adding its four sides, 48 inches + 48 inches + 40 inches + 40 inches = 176 inches.

Can you estimate how many boxes are in the back of this truck? Count to see if you were right. Do you think your parents' truck could fit this many boxes? No way!

Conversion Box
1 inch = 2.5 centimeters
1 square inch = 6.5 square centimeters

The **area** of a pallet is found by multiplying its length and width, 48 inches x 40 inches = 1,920 square inches. The area of a grocery bag is 14 inches x 12 inches = 168 square inches. 1,920 square inches > 168 square inches. One pallet could hold a lot of grocery bags!

If a truck can fit 10 pallets, each with 20 boxes on it, how many boxes can the truck carry? The math sentence is: 10 x 20 = 200 boxes.

What is the perimeter of a grocery bag that measures 14 inches long and 12 inches wide?

(See answers on p. 22)

Figure It Out

How Far Is It?

You are going to a sleepover and your friend's dad picks you up in his monster truck. You find out that it is 10,487 feet from your house to your friend's house.

To figure out how far that is in miles, first know that there are 5,280 feet in a mile. Dividing 10,487 by 5,280 will tell you the number of miles it is to your friend's house. However, 10,487 and 5,280 are difficult numbers to divide. Instead you can estimate.

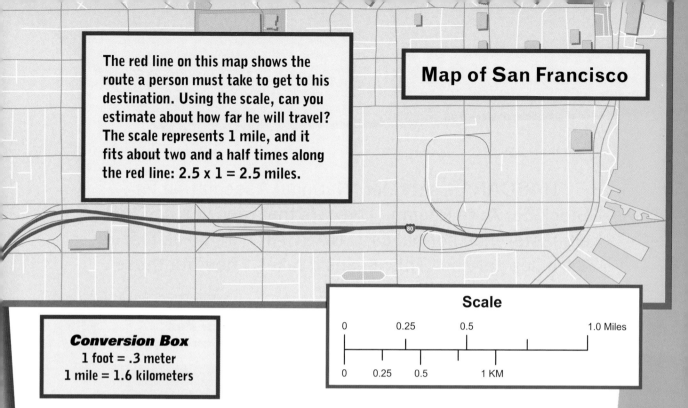

The red line on this map shows the route a person must take to get to his destination. Using the scale, can you estimate about how far he will travel? The scale represents 1 mile, and it fits about two and a half times along the red line: 2.5 x 1 = 2.5 miles.

Map of San Francisco

Conversion Box
1 foot = .3 meter
1 mile = 1.6 kilometers

Scale

| 0 | 0.25 | 0.5 | 1.0 Miles |

| 0 | 0.25 | 0.5 | 1 KM |

A good and approximate guess is that it is 10,000 feet ÷ 5,000 feet per mile = 2 miles to your friend's house. If you did the real math, you would get 1.98 miles. Your estimate got you pretty close!

Figure It Out

A kilometer equals 1,000 meters. Estimate how many kilometers are about equal to 4,134 meters. Round down to make the math easier!

(See answers on p. 22)

How Long Will It Take?

"NASCAR" is short for "National Association for Stock Car Auto Racing." The cars that race in NASCAR are faster than normal cars. NASCAR cars go as fast as 200 miles per hour. This means it takes 1 hour for these cars to drive 200 miles.

Conversion Box
1 mile per hour = 1.6 kilometers per hour

You will not be able to drive as fast on a rough road like this one as you would on a highway. If you drove for 3 hours on this road and you went 25 miles per hour, you would travel
3 hours x 25 miles per hour = 75 miles.

A car enters a race that is 400 miles long and the driver races at 200 miles per hour. Miles divided by speed equals the time the car has driven:
400 miles ÷ 200 miles per hour = 2 hours.
It takes the driver 2 hours to finish the race.

Figure It Out

If you go on vacation and travel 300 kilometers while driving 100 kilometers per hour, how many hours does the trip take?

(See answers on p. 22)

Tire Math

A pizza is a circle that is cut into parts. The space between the lines or edges of a slice of pizza is an **angle**. Similarly, the wheels of a car are a circle and you can look at the parts. Below is a wheel with a hubcap on it that has six parts.

This truck's wheel is divided into 6 triangular pieces. Circles always have 360 degrees, so you can divide by 6 to find out the angle in each piece: 360 degrees ÷ 6 = 60 degrees.

Degrees are a unit of measure for circles. There are 360 degrees in a circle. The sum of the six parts of the wheel is 360 degrees. Each part, or angle, is 360 degrees ÷ 6 = 60 degrees.

This wheel is divided into five triangular pieces, so each angle is 360 degrees ÷ 5 = 72 degrees. You are getting great at figuring out angles on circles!

The hubcaps of an RV split each wheel into eight parts. How many degrees is each angle that is made by the hubcaps?

(See answers on p. 22)

Figure It Out

Park the Car

Four **Formula 1** racecars come to a party at Sam's house. The cars are each 15 feet long and park in the driveway, which is 60 feet long. There is a wall at the end of the driveway, and the first car parks 1 foot from it. The other cars park 1 foot behind the car ahead. A diagram or number line can help you describe a word problem like this one.

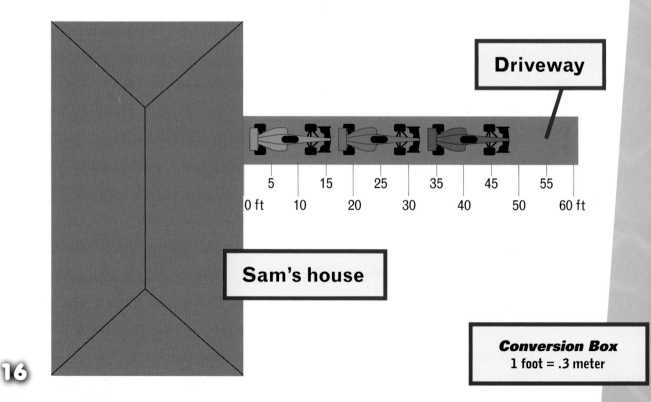

Driveway

5   15   25   35   45   55

0 ft   10   20   30   40   50   60 ft

Sam's house

Conversion Box
1 foot = .3 meter

The length of three cars parked in the driveway is 48 feet. The remaining length of driveway is 60 feet – 48 feet = 12 feet. A fourth car will not fit in that space.

If three rows of three cars can fit in this driveway, then nine cars will fit: 3 x 3 = 9.

How many moving trucks that are 25 feet long fit in a driveway 50 feet long? The first truck parks 1 foot from the wall, and the rest of the trucks park with 1 foot between them.

Figure It Out

(See answers on p. 22)

The Ice Cream Truck

Some ice cream trucks scoop ice cream from 3-**gallon** containers and serve the ice cream on cones. A gallon is a measure of **volume**.

An ice cream truck has three 3-gallon containers of chocolate ice cream, and each gallon makes 32 cones. Now we can figure out how many cones the truck can serve. A container has 3 gallons. To find how many cones each container makes, we would write: 3 gallons x 32 cones per gallon = 96 cones. There are three containers in the truck, so the math sentence to find the number of cones the truck can make is: 3 containers x 96 cones per container = 288 ice cream cones. Let's find that truck!

Conversion Box
1 gallon = 3.8 liters

Can you estimate how many scoops of ice cream will be served to these 10 children in line? If you guess each cone likely has two or three scoops, there will be somewhere between 20 and 30 scoops served.

CROSS
AT
REAR

This Truck is Available for
Private Parties and Outings.
Please ask the Driver for Details.

An ice cream truck has six 3-gallon containers of ice cream. How many ice cream cones can the truck serve?

(See answers on p. 22)

Figure It Out

Math Is Everywhere

Math is everywhere. Cars and trucks can help you learn a lot about estimating and measuring. There are many other **vehicles** that can help you with math, too.

There are many things to measure on a train. If a train has eight cars and each car is 75 feet long, the train is

75 feet per car x 8 cars = 600 feet long.

You can measure the length, width, and height of motorcycles. Motorcycles also contain liquids like gasoline. You can measure the volume of gasoline. Can you think of more things to measure in other vehicles?

Conversion Box
1 foot = .3 meter

Formula 1 are very light at only about 1,400 pounds (640 kg), including the driver. Can you estimate how much the car would weigh without a driver? You need to estimate what a driver would weigh, then subtract.

What is the perimeter of a train car that is 60 feet long and 8 feet wide?

(See answers on p. 22)

Figure It Out: The Answers

Page 5: **The truck weighs**
8 tons x 2,000 pounds per ton = 16,000 pounds.

Page 7: **Divide the width of the trunk by the width of one suitcase:**
48 inches ÷ 16 inches = 3 suitcases fit in the trunk.

Page 9: **The perimeter is**
14 inches + 12 inches + 14 inches + 12 inches = 52 inches.

Page 11: **An estimation is**
4,000 meters ÷ 1,000 meters per kilometer = 4 kilometers.

Page 13: **The drive takes**
300 kilometers ÷ 100 kilometers per hour = 3 hours.

Page 15: **The angle is 360 degrees ÷ 8 = 45 degrees.**

Page 17:**The first truck takes up 1 foot + 25 feet = 26 feet of space in the driveway. There is 50 feet – 26 feet = 24 feet left, but that's not enough room for another truck. There is space for only one truck.**

Page 19: **Each container has enough ice cream for 96 cones. Six containers have enough ice cream for:**
6 containers x 96 cones per container = 576 ice cream cones.

Page 21: **The perimeter is**
60 feet + 8 feet + 60 feet + 8 feet = 136 feet.

Glossary

angle (ANG-gul) The space between two lines that come together at a point.

antique (an-TEEK) Made a long time ago.

approximate (uh-PROK-suh-met) Nearly correct.

area (ER-ee-uh) A measure of a space.

degrees (dih-GREEZ) A unit of measure for circles. 1 degree is 1/360 of a circle.

estimate (ES-teh-mayt) To make a guess based on knowledge or facts.

Formula 1 (FAWR-myuh-luh WUN) A type of car racing. The cars have one seat and the wheels are on the outside of the car's body.

gallon (GA-lun) A volume of liquid equal to 4 quarts.

measurement (MEZH-shur-ment) An exact amount found.

pallets (PA-lets) Rectangles made most often of wood used to move groceries or other merchandise.

perimeter (peh-RIH-meh-tur) The outline of a place or thing.

similar (SIH-muh-ler) Almost the same as.

vehicles (VEE-uh-kulz) Objects that move or carry things.

volume (VOL-yoom) The amount of space that something takes up.

Index

Websites

Due to the changing nature of Internet links, PowerKids Press has developed an online list of websites related to the subject of this book. This site is updated regularly. Please use this link to access the list: www.powerkidslinks.com/cms/car/